Rising Parent Media, LLC

© 2018 by Rising Parent Media
All rights reserved. 2nd edition, published 2018
First edition © 2016 by Rising Parent Media
Printed in the United States of America

22 21 20 19 18   2 3 4 5

ISBN: 978-0-9987312-7-8 (paperback)

The paper used in this publication meets the minimum requirements of the American National Standard for Information Sciences—Permanence of Paper for Printed Library Materials, ANSI Z39.48-1992.

www.educateempowerkids.org

FOR GREAT RESOURCES AND INFORMATION, FOLLOW US ON OUR SOCIAL MEDIA OUTLETS:

Facebook: www.facebook.com/educateempowerkids/
Twitter: @EduEmpowerKids
Pinterest: pinterest.com/educateempower/
Instagram: Eduempowerkids

HOW TO TALK TO YOUR KIDS ABOUT PORNOGRAPHY

FOR 6-18 YEAR-OLDS

EDUCATE AND EMPOWER KIDS WOULD LIKE TO ACKNOWLEDGE THE FOLLOWING PEOPLE WHO CONTRIBUTED TIME, TALENTS, AND ENERGY TO THIS PUBLICATION:

Dina Alexander, MS
Amanda Scott
Jenny Webb, MA

Kyle Duran, MA
Tina Mattsson
Ed Allison
Cliff Park, MBA

DESIGN AND ILLUSTRATION BY:
Jera Mehrdad
Jenny Webb, MA

TABLE OF CONTENTS

"NO PARENT CAN CHILD-PROOF THE WORLD. A PARENT'S JOB IS TO WORLD-PROOF THE CHILD."

—DOUG FLANDERS, MD

INTRODUCTION

Because exposure to pornography is inevitable, it's become necessary to prepare our kids for that exposure. Porn's addictive nature, the way it can alter a child's developing brain, and how it will affect all of their future relationships make these discussions not only important, but vital to a child's healthy sexual development. Pornography use among kids is now a major public health issue due to its far-reaching effects.

We have provided critical information and great discussion questions that will foster productive and meaningful conversations between you and your kids. Look at these discussions as an opportunity to grow closer. As you become more comfortable and gain confidence in discussing these tough topics, your kids will be able to ask you deeper questions and share more personal thoughts and experiences with you. You will find that if you can discuss the dangers of online pornography and the related topics in this book, you can talk with your kids about ANYTHING!

This book will also help you determine the particular needs for your home, whether it's clearer standards and guidelines, more monitoring, or more trust and connection. Cultivating a deep connection with our kids is one of the best addiction prevention tools we have. Use these conversations to foster meaningful connection with your kids and help establish your own role as their parent—someone they can trust, someone they can talk to, and someone who will protect them.

1. PORNOGRAPHY: A MAJOR PUBLIC HEALTH ISSUE

"WHEN THE INCREASED ACCESS AND EXCESSIVE USE OF PORNOGRAPHY IS LINKED TO PROBLEMATIC BEHAVIORS, THIS TREND THEN BECOMES A PUBLIC HEALTH ISSUE."

—CORDELIA ANDERSON (2015)

Our kids are becoming entrenched in an increasingly pornified culture (*a trend in culture and human behavior in which media—entertainment, advertising, fashion, pop culture, etc.—is hyper-sexualized resulting from the normalization of pornography use.*)

Pornography is very different today than when we were kids. Gone are the nearly quaint pictorials of naked and partially dressed women that adorned magazines like *Playboy*. "Type 'porn' into Google, and you won't see anything that looks like the old pinups; instead, you will be catapulted into a world of sexual cruelty and brutality, where women are subject to body-punishing sex and called vile names" (Dines, 2015).

EVERY CHILD YOU REACH DESERVES TO BE WARNED ABOUT THE PERILS OF ONLINE PORNOGRAPHY!

Excessive use of pornography is harmful to sexual functioning and development for males and females of any age. A child or teen's exposure to violent or excessive pornography can change a child's brain, social interactions, and emotional skills well into their 20s (Anderson, 2011).

Pornography hurts individuals, families, and society. Facing the epidemic of pornography use is not just for "liberals" or "conservatives." Nor can this problem be viewed through a narrow lens as a "religious" or "feminist" issue—any more than poverty, teen pregnancy, or a measles epidemic can be viewed as such. It is an issue that anyone who cares about children (including par-ents, educators, therapists, and community leaders) needs to be concerned about and willing to act upon.

UNDERSTANDING THIS PUBLIC HEALTH CRISIS: WHY SHOULD I TALK TO MY CHILD ABOUT PORNOGRAPHY

- Pornography is as addictive and as harmful as any drug, and our kids' undeveloped brains are ill-equipped to deal with the violent, damaging content available 24 hours a day/7 days a week.

- As healthy as it is to be curious about sex, it is NOT healthy to use pornography.

- Children need to be aware of the hateful nature of pornography, where women are usually the targets or victims of objectification, violence, degradation, and humiliation. It is also overtly racist, playing up every negative stereotype from a variety of cultures.

- It will help my child and me to be more aware of how easily accessible it is in my home, her school, and his friends' houses.

- She needs time to prepare herself for the oncoming pressure. He needs to recognize dangerous sites and know how to handle it when he is exposed.

THE FACTS

The average age of exposure to pornography is 11-years-old (Weiss, 2015).

A 2010 study of 50 of the most popular adult videos found that 88% contained scenes of physical aggression toward women (including, but not limited to slapping, gagging, and spanking), with the primary target being women and the primary perpetrator being men (Bridges, et al., 2010).

In a 2009 study, 42% of adolescents reported exposure to pornography online with 66% of those teens describing such exposure as unwanted (Braun-Courville, et al., 2009).

Teens with early pornography exposure are significantly more likely to have sex at an earlier age, have oral sex, anal sex, and sex with multiple partners, engage in risky sexual behaviors, view women as sexual objects, and experience increased difficulty in developing intimate relationships with partners (Owens, et al., 2012).

BE THE FIRST, BEST SOURCE OF INFORMATION FOR YOUR KIDS

2. COMMON QUESTIONS

WHAT AGE SHOULD I START THESE DISCUSSIONS?

We believe in starting these discussions with a child between the ages of three and four, however the discussions in this book are meant for kids ages 6–18. If your child has access to an internet-enabled device in your home or any place he or she spends time, they need to be warned about potential dangers. If you feel the discussions in this book are too mature for your younger children, please visit our website at http://educateempowerkids.org/resources/ for a starter lesson on Teaching Your Child About Pornography (Ages 3–7).

WHAT TOPICS SHOULD I ADDRESS FIRST?

- It is important that your child first understand that curiosity is normal and that a desire for knowledge of sexual matters is healthy.

- Next she should know what pornography is.

- Then a plan should be established for how to deal with future exposure.

- After that, you should adjust your "chats" to fit your child's needs including, but not limited to, discussions of intimacy (the opposite of pornography), addiction, media literacy, self-monitoring, and the other topics in this book are vital. We intentionally put the most important topics in this book!

SHOULD I DO THESE CONVERSATIONS ONE-ON-ONE? OR WITH MY KIDS TOGETHER?

Most topics should be covered one-one-one, at least at first. As your kids become more comfortable with these topics, you may find that a group discussion breeds better discussion. Remember, you know your children best. Watch their non-verbal cues. Is he or she squirming with discomfort, having trouble meeting your eye, or trying to run out of the room? If he or she is uncomfortable, put your child at ease by reassuring him that you love him and that although it may be awkward, this is a very important issue to talk about.

IF MY CHILD IS UNCOMFORTABLE, SHOULD I STOP?

No. However, you need to find the source of their discomfort and address it. Keep in mind, if your child were uncomfortable talking about heroin and there were a drug dealer living on your street, you would still need to talk about it. Pornography is like a drug, and there is a "dealer" in every internet-enabled device within her reach. Ultimately you know your child best, and as you start these talks, you will know with which topics to proceed with, and which ones to postpone.

SHOULD I TACKLE SEVERAL TOPICS TOGETHER?

Not at first. Begin simply. You should start with one topic and cover two to four points that you feel are most important. Ask the questions at the end of each lesson that you are comfortable ask-ing and be prepared to listen. After that, build upon the foundation you have established. Following up with more information is critical to setting yourself up as their "go-to" source for information about media, pornography, and sexual intimacy.

Like most parenting jobs, this is not one you can just check off. Your child will continually be bombarded with hyper-sexualized media throughout her life, and she will be under great pressure to watch porn when she leaves your home.

3. BUILDING A FOUNDATION OF TRUST

Your home and family can be likened to being part of a team, having a shared identity you belong to. When a child knows he has the backing of his "team" to support him, he is more likely to stand up for his convictions, maintain the ideals he has been taught, and communicate more openly at home about his troubles.

Creating an environment of trust at home is critical to emotional development. Children who feel safe at home know they can always count on family and home to provide an emotionally safe place where they can be themselves, express feelings, and know they are loved—all without fear of ridicule and neglect.

- -

THE FOLLOWING GUIDELINES ARE VITAL TO CREATE THIS ENVIRONMENT

- -

MAKE HOME A REFUGE FROM THE STORMS OF LIFE

As kids get older they often feel like they must be on their guard at school or in their social lives. They spend their time in shifting environments and with people who may or may not accept them. Make your home a place where they know they can trust those around them to support them in times of need. Create a home where the standards are known and fully understood.

HAVE ROUTINE AND STRUCTURE

Kids will look to home during times of emotional uncertainty or instability in other parts of their lives in order to help them feel safe and secure. Home should be a place where things are reliable and as balanced as possible.

HAVE STANDARDS AND RULES FOR YOUR KIDS

Your kids rely on you, as the parent, to protect them and prepare them. When you set expectations, kids will often push against these boundaries, providing you with a great teaching opportunity. Children should know, however, that if a mistake is made or a rule broken, that there will be consequences, but also that your response will be appropriate and predictable—without screaming or physical harm.

LOOK FOR OPPORTUNITIES TO BE POSITIVE

Greet children with love and a smile. Find ways to daily compliment your kids and your partner. Teach them to reciprocate this behavior to you. With so much negativity at school, work, and in the media, your positivity will go a long way in emotionally fortifying your family members.

AVOID USING SHAME

Using shame to teach about sex or pornography, or using shame when we confront our kids about their porn use is disastrous. As you use this book your child should see porn use as making a serious mistake (he or she may feel guilt if they choose to use it) but NOT in terms of identification as "I am a bad person if I use porn" (feeling shame for its use). Your child will not come to you with future concern about pornography (or other issues) if you use shame to approach these talks.

Examples of teaching kids about pornography using shame:

- "Anyone who looks at pornography is perverted!"

- "How could you look at something so disgusting?"

- "How do you think it makes me feel when you do that?"

Any discussion you have with your child about pornography should lead to positive notions about healthy sexuality. Keep in mind it's crucial to convey that sex is not bad, dirty, or shameful. Create a healthy atmosphere that values sex as beautiful and amazing.

> **WHEN ONE FEELS GUILTY THEY MAY SAY, "I MADE A MISTAKE" OR "I REALLY MESSED UP."**
>
> **WHEN ONE FEELS SHAME THEY MAY SAY, "I AM A TERRIBLE PERSON." "I DON'T DESERVE FORGIVENESS."**

LOOK AT THESE TALKS AS AN OPPORTUNITY TO GROW CLOSER TOGETHER

Once you have gone through a few of these talks, your children will grow more comfortable and feel able to ask you deeper questions and share personal thoughts and experiences more readily with you. Sharing and creating deeper conversations builds a foundation of closeness and trust.

4. CREATING A HOME OF OPENNESS

THE SAFE ZONE

You may want to create a "safe zone" in your home when discussing these or other tough topics. **During a "safe zone" conversation, your child should feel free and safe to ask any questions or make any comments without judgment or repercussion. She should be able to use the term "safe zone" again when she wants to discuss, confide, or consult with you about tough subjects.**

It is never too early and never too late to set habits and show a great example of tolerance, acceptance, and openness. Ultimately, we are trying to create a home environment based on trust where your child knows he can ask you ANYTHING! This is accomplished by being sensitive and nonjudgmental. Here are some steps to help you establish and promote openness in your home.

BE CALM

Many parents experience anxiety or fear when discussing sex or pornography with their kids. First, take your emotional level down when discussing these topics. Be calm and matter-of-fact during these conversations. If you are calm, your kids will be calm.

USE YOUR CULTURAL, PERSONAL, AND SPIRITUAL VALUES TO GUIDE THESE DISCUSSIONS

If you think porn is something that is okay for adults to look at, but not kids, tell your kids—but explain why you think this. If you have religious objections to pornography, discuss this. If you feel that pornography is a vicious, misogynistic expression of corporatization, then focus on this.

SHARE PERSONAL EXPERIENCES

Share both the positive and negative experiences you've had. A child will be more receptive if he or she can attach a real life experience to the discussion. For example, you may wish to talk about the first time you were exposed to pornography (without being too graphic) or share the difficulties of someone you know whose life has been impacted by pornography. Make sure the example is appropriate to the age, experience, and maturity of the child.

PRACTICE ACTIVE LISTENING

As you ask your kids the discussion questions, pay attention to their words, facial expressions, and other body language. Show your kids you are listening by validating what they ask or say and by sometimes repeating back or paraphrasing what you have heard.

USE FACTS AND SCIENCE TO DISCUSS THE DANGERS

Use this opportunity to explain how addiction works and how pornography can literally change a brain (see 9. Pornography is Addictive). Also, take time to review the social science research (see 10. Pornography Conditions the Brain and 22. Porn Destroys) that tells us how exposure to pornography at a young age changes one's perceptions and beliefs about sex and relationships, increases violence toward women, and promotes rape culture.

BE PREPARED FOR AWESOME DISCUSSIONS

One great benefit from these difficult conversations is excellent discussions with your kids. It may not happen with the first or second chat, but very soon, your child will ask you some pretty amazing questions. When you approach tough topics with your child, together, as a team, you will develop a sense of camaraderie and a feeling that you are in this together. This closeness will open the door for other, deeper conversations that will continue to strengthen your relationship.

YOUR ATTITUDE SHOULD BE ONE OF CARING AND LOVE

Through your words and actions, convey to your child how much you care about him. Explain why you want to educate and prepare him. This will convey more than any words you say. Your child may not remember everything you discuss from this book, but she will remember the caring (or lack thereof) behind the words.

5. WHERE DO I START?

FIRST, FOCUS ON YOUR END GOAL

What do you want your child to get out of these conversations? Do you want your child to be unafraid? To be informed? To be prepared? Write your end goal and your plan somewhere that you can revisit during this process. Let your goal guide you as you decide what the focus of your talks will be and what questions to ask.

Think about what YOU want to get out of these conversations. Do you want to build your relationship with your child? Do you want to have intellectually stimulating conversations? Do you want to ensure that your child is prepared for the experiences they will have with porn? Think about what kind of experience you and your child will have together. Will this be interesting to both of you? Awkward? Serious? You will set the tone! Your voice, comfort level, and demeanor will establish the feeling of these talks.

DECIDE TOGETHER WHICH TOPICS NEED TO BE ADDRESSED FIRST

If possible, have a discussion between you and your partner. If you can approach this topic as a team, you will be more successful. We understand that many of you have a partner who may use pornography. Use your best judgment when approaching sensitive topics. Think of how you can talk openly with your child about the dangers of pornography without vilifying your partner (or ex-partner). Look through the Table of Contents and decide which topic should come first.

ACCEPT THAT YOU WILL NOT BE PERFECT

Letting go of perfection will make the whole process easier and more enjoyable! Your child does not expect perfection from you; she expects understanding and love. If your child asks you some-thing that you do not have the answer to, be honest and tell her that you don't know. Then take the time to find the answer and report back to your child.

HEAL YOURSELF

If you find these discussions intimidating or triggering due to past sexual abuse or other trauma, get help. Talk with a trusted friend or therapist. Your child is worth the effort, and so are you!

YOUR CHILD DOES NOT EXPECT PERFECTION FROM YOU; SHE EXPECTS UNDERSTANDING AND LOVE.

BE REALISTIC IN YOUR APPROACH

Know that all of our children will be exposed to pornography. Instead of approaching the discussion as "This is something you might see someday," inform and prepare your child by letting them know, "This is something you will see at some point."

PLAN EACH TALK AHEAD OF TIME, BUT DO NOT CREATE AN "EVENT"

Take a few minutes to think about what you want to say, but don't go overboard. Why not? Because you want your child to be able to recreate this event every time he has a question for you. And if he feels like he can only ask questions once a year during a big "event," he may go seeking his own answers from other sources. Make the discussions so commonplace that your child knows they can come to you at any time when a question comes up.

BE AN EXAMPLE

Pornography teaches that mutual respect and empathy are irrelevant and that women (and sometimes men) are not worthy of equality or kindness. By showing respect to people of all races, nationalities, or genders, demonstrating self-respect, and modeling strong relationships, we can confront these falsehoods.

TAKE TIME TO INVENTORY YOUR OWN BEHAVIORS!

EXAMINE YOUR LIFE:—DO MY VIEWING HABITS AND MUSIC CHOICES AFFECT HOW I VIEW THE WORLD OR INTERACT WITH OTHERS?

- Do I watch movies with pornographic language or images?
- Do I listen to sexually explicit music?
- Do I use derogatory or sexually demeaning language? How might this impact my children?
- Do I use sexual language casually?

6. DEFINING PORNOGRAPHY

It can be difficult to define pornography when aspects of it are all around us. Images once deemed too explicit or improper are now the wallpaper of our pornified culture. Think for a moment about the billboards, mall window displays, magazines at the grocery checkout, television commercials, and movies available to us and our children. Music and books containing thematic content that emphasizes how a woman or girl should offer herself up sexually are increasingly being sold to children and teens. Boys are taught that the hyper-masculine, overly-muscular, aggressive male is the ideal.

But none of these seem to compare with the brutal depictions of sex available on any smart phone or other internet enabled device. It is important that you understand what the new definition of pornography is! Pornography can no longer be defined in terms of Playboy or Hustler magazines. Kids aren't seeking out magazines. Kids may stumble upon or seek out sexual imagery online by googling certain terms or searching the word "porn," but they are immediately exposed to videos of hardcore pornography.

📖 **Pornography:** *The portrayal of* **explicit sexual content for the purpose or intent of causing sexual arousal.** *In it,* **sex and bodies are commodified** *(made into a product for sale) for the purpose of making a financial profit.*

*It is important to note that pornography is not made for the purpose of educating others or creating art. It is made and distributed to make money.

OTHER DEFINITIONS THAT MAY HELP YOUR CHILD UNDERSTAND WHAT PORNOGRAPHY IS:

- Pornography is pictures or videos of people with little or no clothes on.
- Online pornography usually shows videos of people having sex.
- It shows private actions in order to make money.

It can be daunting to face the realities of our pornified culture, but you can use every-day examples all around you (both positive and the negative) to teach your kids your expectations and your beliefs. Research tells us that your influence as parents can be much stronger than any other influences if you can begin talking and continue these discussions throughout your child's time at home (Kemmet, n.d.).

WHAT IS YOUR CHILD BEING SOCIALIZED INTO BY POP CULTURE?

Girls: *Their value lies in their looks and sexual availability.*

Boys: *Their value lies in hyper-masculine looks and dominating behavior.*

Both: *Women/girls are supposed to be sexually available at all times.*

One does not need a relationship to have sex and it requires no intimacy.

That the opposite gender is less than theirs.

DISCUSSION QUESTIONS

What makes something pornographic?

Have you ever seen pornography?

What is the difference between art and pornography?

What is the significance of a person's body being commodified (made into a sellable product)? Is this wrong?

What do we mean by a "pornified" culture? Can you see examples of a pornified culture around you?

7. CURIOSITY IS NORMAL

Children have a natural curiosity about their bodies and the way they function. Think of the first time you opened your child's diaper only to have him grab himself. Such actions are innate and perfectly normal.

The older our kids get, the more curious they become, and the more questions they have. As a parent, it is a huge mistake to avoid these questions or give answers like "I'll explain when you're older."

GETTING PAST OUR OWN ISSUES WITH SEX

It can be difficult to talk about sex and things related to it if we have our own hang-ups about the subject. Try hard to address the topic positively and head on. If you are embarrassed by your child's curiosity and questions, you imply there is something shameful about these topics. However, if you answer your child's questions openly and honestly, you demonstrate that sexuality is positive and that healthy relationships are something to seek when the time is right.

VALIDATE AND MAKE YOUR CHILD FEEL AS COMFORTABLE AS POSSIBLE

It's so important that children never be made to feel embarrassed for being curious. It's completely natural. As tough as it may be, validate your child's awareness and answer questions honestly and completely. Try to make your child feel as comfortable as possible when he or she comes to you with questions.

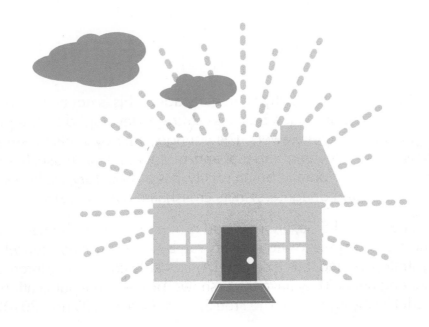

SEEKING OUT ANSWERS

If your child comes to you and confesses seeking out pornography due to curiosity, congratulate yourself: your child trusts you enough to be honest. Second, reassure your child that curiosity and questions about sex and bodies are normal, but that porn isn't where your child should be finding their answers. Remind your child that you will always be honest with them and can answer any questions he or she might have a lot better than pornography can. You should also reassure your child that it is normal to be become aroused when viewing pornography—that is its intent.

Before you begin, ask yourself a few of these questions: How can we as parents feel more comfortable talking about these things ourselves? How can we learn to recognize questions our kids may not feel comfortable asking? (He or she may ask "test" questions to assess your comfort with the questions they actually have). How will you teach your child that, although we are all sexual beings, we all have control over our actions?

DISCUSSION QUESTIONS

Why is it natural to be curious about sex?

What is a productive and healthy way of finding out answers to questions about sex?

What can I do as your Mom/Dad to help you feel comfortable coming to me for any and every question you might have about your body?

8. AN ADULT INDUSTRY TARGETING KIDS

Today, kids are exposed to pornography at an early age. "This is not an unfortunate by-product of easily accessible porn, but a business strategy developed by the porn industry to attract younger and younger viewers. The younger the boy starts masturbating to porn, the more likely he is to develop habitual and/or addictive porn use. Porn is often misleadingly defined as fun or fantasy, but in reality, it is a predatory, multi-billion dollar industry that has our sons (and daughters) in its crosshairs" (Dines, 2015).

The porn industry is not a small-time, unorganized group of people who have made billions by sheer luck. It is a sophisticated industry run by savvy businessmen who create brilliant marketing strategies, and interface with banks, cable companies, Internet providers, and software engineers. They have trade shows, professional publications, awards shows, and a powerful lobbying group, The Free Speech Coalition (Dines, 2010).

> "PORN IS OFTEN MISLEADINGLY DEFINED AS FUN OR FANTASY, BUT IN REALITY, IT IS A PREDATORY, MULTI-BILLION DOLLAR INDUSTRY THAT HAS OUR SONS (AND DAUGHTERS) IN ITS CROSSHAIRS."
> —GAIL DINES

This powerful industry with incredible political clout is worth approximately $97 billion dollars worldwide (Morris, 2015). Within the United States, they are worth more than all major league sports and Hollywood combined (about $13 billion dollars). With this financial and political power, it has successfully woven itself seamlessly into pop culture, selling itself as a fun, cool, harmless adventure. This success, however, is founded on poor regulation, deplorable working conditions for its workers, predatory methods for obtaining women, and extremely limited options for women to be involved in any production capacity (see 24. The Trafficking Connection).

Porn's indiscriminate accessibility, use of cartoon/manga genres, the industry's target marketing to youth-centered social media like Snapchat and Instagram, and its refusal to do anything to stop kids from seeing or consuming its products online are just part of the evidence that this industry is actively angling for our children's hearts, minds, and future dollars. Targeting children with 'free' or sample videos is one way to get them hooked as lifelong customers. Over time the user needs more intense, hardcore material to achieve the same level of sexual arousal and satisfaction—that is where the paid subscriptions come into play (Alexander 2016).

DISCUSSION QUESTIONS

What is the goal of the porn industry?

Why is it wrong for an industry to target kids with websites and videos that are only legal for adults to watch?

Is it problematic for an industry to dictate the sexual desires and appetites of people (much like corporations have dictated the eating habits of billions of people)?

Should the porn industry or the government create regulations that protect kids from pornography (such as requiring people to prove they are 18 years old before allowing them on pornographic websites)? Or should parents be solely responsible for what kids consume in and out of their homes?

Free speech is an integral part of many cultures.

Should an industry have the freedom to say or produce anything it wants?

Why are some products legal when they cause harm to us (like cigarettes, sugary foods, pornography)?

9. PORNOGRAPHY IS ADDICTIVE

All of us have a reward circuit in our brains. This circuit is activated when we engage in behaviors that further our survival (having sex, eating, bonding, experiencing novelty). Within the circuit is the brain's reward center (the nucleus accumbens). Some substances and behaviors that are actually damaging to a person also stimulate the brain's reward circuit and reward center.

It is here that drug and alcohol use, and porn use, boost dopamine, a neurotransmitter that helps produce pleasurable feelings, thus prompting more cravings. In order to satiate these strong cravings, a user will return to the behaviors that gave them that initial blast of dopamine.

As these behaviors are repeated, new pathways are created in this reward circuit to make it easier for dopamine to be released and travel along the path. Think of it like a mountain trail. The more a person uses it, the more worn and the deeper the grooves in the earth are. Scientists refer to this phenomenon—this changing of the brain—as neuroplasticity, in which the brain is continually laying down new pathways based on one's experiences (Wilson, 2015).

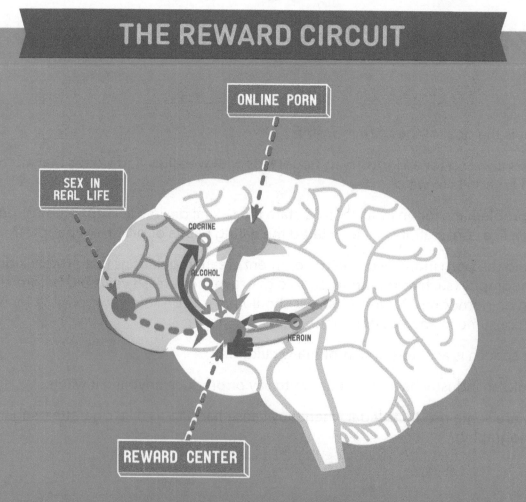

THE REWARD CIRCUIT

ONLINE PORN

SEX IN REAL LIFE

COCAINE

ALCOHOL

HEROIN

REWARD CENTER

These deepening pathways are the physical evidence of tolerance. As a user becomes more tolerant, he needs more variety and more hardcore porn to get the "high" or sexual release they received from earlier porn use. This is how people can easily progress to viewing porn that used to shock or disgust them. Eventually, the person becomes addicted and craves pornography even when he no longer even "likes" it.

Children's and teens' brains are much more susceptible to dopamine and this addiction process ("Pitt Researchers Find," 2011)! Therefore a child or teen brain can change more readily and is more susceptible to the addictive effects of pornography.

> **SOME SUBSTANCES AND BEHAVIORS THAT ARE ACTUALLY DAMAGING TO A PERSON ALSO STIMULATE THE BRAIN'S REWARD CIRCUIT AND REWARD CENTER.**

DISCUSSION QUESTIONS

How does addiction work?

If pornography can change your brain or hook you into an addiction, why do some people still use it?

If you look at pornography one time, will you get addicted?

Why do some people get addicted or porn, food, or alcohol when others do not?

Why can't someone just stop using porn when he or she wants to? Why can't people just ignore cravings?

Some people seek out pornography when tired, bored, lonely, sad, or stressed out. What do you do when you have these types of feelings? How do you cope?

What are some things we can do to avoid a pornography addiction? What are some other activities we can do when we feel bored, lonely or sad?

10. PORNOGRAPHY CONDITIONS THE BRAIN

Internet pornography provides what is known as a supra normal stimulus, a term coined by Nikolaas Tinbergen in 1951. He and current evolutionary biologists use the term to describe any stimulus that elicits a response stronger than the stimulus for which it evolved, even if it is artificial. Some examples of this supra normal stimuli include processed, sugary or high sodium foods, video games, illegal drugs, and pornography (Ciotti, 2014).

In his experiments, Tinbergen constructed cardboard dummy butterflies with more defined markings that male butterflies would try to mate with in preference to real female butterflies.

He also found that male stickleback fish would attack a wooden fish model more vigorously than a real male if its underside was more red. Finally, he painted plaster eggs to see which one a bird preferred to sit on, and found that the birds would pick those that were larger, more saturated with color, and had more defined markings. They would even reject their own, pale, dappled eggs in favor of the false eggs (Ciotti, 2014).

Tinbergen was able to influence the behavior of these animals using a "super" stimulus, just as pornography today influences kids and adults to prefer unrealistic, surgically-enhanced, or even photo-shopped versions of people. Kids are being conditioned to prefer the limitless supply of novelty in porn to actual females (Hilton, 2015).

📖 **Rape Myth:** *The belief that women are responsible for rape, like rape, want rape, and that there are few negative consequences for rape.*

PORN CHANGES OUR BELIEFS AND ATTITUDES

As we consume various images and media, they seep into our subconscious, creating new ideas as they change our expectations and become our beliefs. As Gail Dines said, "images construct the way we think in the world. They jump off the pages and into our lives, our identities and our sexuality" (Dines, 2012).

In an extensive review of the current research, it was found that adolescent porn users were more likely to have sex at a younger age, have attitudes that support violence against women, develop compulsive internet use, and engage in risky sexual behavior (Owens, et. al, 2012).

Other research of adult male porn users suggests that users are more likely to rate their partners as less attractive, view women as sex objects, sexually harass women, sexually abuse partners, and believe the Rape Myth (the belief that women are responsible for rape, like rape, want rape, and that there are few negative consequences for rape) (Layden, 2004).

DISCUSSION QUESTIONS

Have you ever seen a commercial on a hot, summer day for a cold beverage? Did you suddenly realize you were thirsty and needed something to drink right away?

Have you ever heard a news story on the radio and then watched a similar news story online or on the television? Did seeing the images of the incident affect how you experienced the story? (An example of this is seeing the destruction caused by a natural disaster such as a hurricane or earthquake. When we see these images, we tend to feel more empathy and concern for those who have lost loved ones or lost their home.) How might we FEEL and THINK differently after seeing an image or video of people versus just hearing about it?

Some people argue that using pornography does not affect their attitude, or how they think in any way. If this is true, then why do we have commercials for fast food, new cars, and beauty prod-ucts? Why do corporations spend billions on advertising in order to influence us to buy their products?

Is it possible to be immune to repeated porn use? Can you repeatedly watch porn and have it NOT affect your thoughts? Your fantasies? The way you view women (and men)? Your expectations of sex?

11. IF YOUR CHILD HAS BEEN EXPOSED TO PORNOGRAPHY

How will YOU handle it? Your reaction and subsequent follow up conversations are vital. If you don't discuss it in a proactive and sensitive way, your child may not trust you enough to come to you when it happens again. The first thing to do is take a deep breath. This might be a tough conversation, but it doesn't have to be. There are specific concrete, positive actions you can teach your child in response that lessen the impact.

DISCUSSION QUESTIONS

These questions will help you determine if your child has experienced a one-time exposure or has formed a habit of using pornography.

Where did you first see pornography?

How did it make you feel?

Have you felt the urge to seek it out again?

What questions do you have about what you saw?

PLAN FOR PARENTS

STAY CALM

Don't lose your cool. Your child is unlikely to keep listening if you start off by screaming, "You saw WHAT?" when you find out that your child has seen porn. It's important to keep a conversational tone.

ASK HOW IT HAPPENED

"Help me understand" is a great way to ask how the exposure occurred.

ASK WHAT YOUR CHILD HAS SEEN

You can take away the secrecy and power of the images your child has seen by dissecting them. Try to help your child understand how unrealistic porn is, but also how dangerous it is to those whose concepts of love and intimacy are influenced by it. Also make your child aware of porn's addictive nature (see 9. Pornography is Addictive).

REASSURE YOUR CHILD THAT CURIOSITY IS NORMAL BUT PORN ISN'T AN ACCURATE REPRESENTATION OF SEX OR LOVE

Yes, porn involves sex. But your child needs to know that porn is not what intimacy is really about. Porn does not contain love, healthy relationships, or positive emotions. Point out to your child that true intimacy—healthy intimacy—should involve all of these qualities.

REMEMBER NOT TO USE SHAME

Avoid shaming your child in an attempt to try to convince your child not to look at it again. Shame and guilt feed into the secretive nature of porn. If a child is made to feel guilty or ashamed of himself, his self-esteem will suffer, which could drive him right back to the porn for a fix.

FORMULATE A PLAN

Decide as a family what to do if confronted with or tempted to look at porn (see 12. What to do When You See Pornography).

FOLLOW UP FREQUENTLY

The older your child gets, the more he or she won't be under your direct supervision. Let your child know YOU haven't forgotten the discussions you've had and that you are always available for follow-up questions. This is the best way to keep the lines of communication open and ensure your child knows you are dependable. No plan is foolproof; no parent is perfect. The most important thing is that you TALK about it. Ignoring it won't make it go away and could very well create or feed into a serious problem.

> **THE MOST IMPORTANT THING IS THAT YOU TALK ABOUT IT. IGNORING IT WON'T MAKE IT GO AWAY AND COULD VERY WELL CREATE OR FEED INTO A SERIOUS PROBLEM.**

12. WHAT TO DO WHEN YOU SEE PORNOGRAPHY

TELL YOUR PARENTS

As soon as you have seen something pornographic, tell a parent (or another trusted adult)! Even if you feel embarrassed or if you have never talked about sex with your parents before, they will want to help you.

DISCUSS YOUR FEELINGS

It's natural to have physical reactions to pornographic images, and even become sexually aroused or excited. But it's also normal to feel disgust, anger, fear, confusion, and curiosity. It can be too much to handle alone, so tell your parents how you are feeling. Let them help you sort it out.

OFFER INFORMATION

Tell your parents how you found it. Curiosity about sex can lead you to look for information about it, many times running into more porn. It could also lead you to actively look for porn. It's natural to be curious, but there are better ways to learn (Stiffelman, 2011).

DECONSTRUCT IMAGES

Talk with your parents about issues of consent, emotions, intimacy, and arousal as seen—or not seen—in pornography (Rosenzweig, 2013). Pornography does not show healthy sexuality, real consent, honest emotions, true intimacy, or natural arousal.

R-U-N PLAN FOR KIDS

RECOGNIZE WHAT YOU'VE SEEN AND GET AWAY FROM IT.

UNDERSTAND WHAT YOU'VE SEEN AND TALK ABOUT HOW IT MADE YOU FELL WITH A TRUSTED ADULT

NEVER SEEK IT OUT AGAIN

COMMUNICATE OPENLY

Continue talking about the effects of porn and its opposite, healthy intimacy and relationships. In the days and weeks following your exposure to porn, be aware of changes in yourself, like increased anger, curiosity, or sadness, and keep talking with your parents about them.

EMPOWER YOURSELF WITH TOOLS TO PREVENT MORE EXPOSURE

The Internet is saturated in porn, and that's not going to change. You and your parents can prevent further exposure, by addressing the technology that enables access and the human emotions that can lead to encounters (such as curiosity, desire, etc.).

WORKING TOGETHER: HAVE A PLAN TO R-U-N

RECOGNIZE WHAT YOU'VE SEEN AND GET AWAY FROM IT

Be able to name it when you see it. There are key things to look for like nudity and obscene noises that can help you identify porn quickly.

Role-play: What will YOU do when you're exposed?

Situation: (Kids) You're at a friend's house and he or she wants to show you something on their computer. After a minute, you recognize that it is pornography. Some things you might say: "This isn't cool, turn it off!" or "That's gross, and I don't want to see it!"

Situation: (Teens) You're with a friend and he or she takes out his cell phone to show you something. It's porn. You could say: "You know that's not how sex really is, right?" or "Stuff like this is degrading to women AND men."

Come up with your own words and a plan so you feel prepared!

UNDERSTAND WHAT YOU'VE SEEN AND TALK ABOUT HOW IT MADE YOU FEEL WITH A TRUSTED ADULT

You may think you're not affected by what you've seen but it truly is an anxiety-inducing experience. Talking about it with your parents (its skewed version of sex, the way it makes one feel, etc.) will take away the mysterious, secretive nature of it, which takes away some of its power.

NEVER SEEK IT OUT AGAIN

Know where you'll be exposed to it and which friends watch it. If you can't persuade your friends not to look at it, then question whether you want to hang out with those friends.

13. DETERMINING IF YOUR CHILD HAS A HABIT OR AN ADDICTION TO PORNOGRAPHY

Addiction: *Dependence on a habit, practice, or habit-forming substance to the extent that its cessation causes trauma.*

After first exposure, some kids will go from occasional use, to a habit, to a full-blown addiction. Each of these levels of use needs to be addressed in its own way. Not all habits are an addiction and some kids are more susceptible to addictive tendencies than others. Due to the nature of addiction and the extraordinary neuroplasticity of the teenage brain, however, a habit can easily become an addiction. As you try to determine the severity of your child's habit, use the following questions to guide you.

FAMILY INVENTORY

(These discussion questions will help you determine if your child is addicted and/or the depth of the addiction.)

When was the last time you saw pornography?

Where is an easy place for you to access pornography?

How often do you watch pornography?

When do you feel the need to view pornography? (When you are feeling bored, angry, frustrated? Porn addiction often comes from using porn as a coping mechanism.)

Do you think porn use is an okay habit?

Has your porn use become an everyday (or multiple times per day) habit?

Does your porn use ever feel out of control?

WAYS TO DETERMINE WHETHER YOUR CHILD HAS A HABIT VERSUS AN ADDICTION

If you look at the history on your child's devices and find pornographic sites, this is an obvious indication that your child is viewing pornography on a regular basis. Determine the regularity and extent to which your child is involved in porn use.

SIGNS THAT YOUR CHILD HAS DEVELOPED A HABIT

- Hiding the phone or device
- Device history containing porn sites
- Everyday language becomes more sexualized
- Jokes about sex/sexualized language
- Inappropriate sexual knowledge for their age
- Increase in contempt/disdainful comments, objectifying others, etc.

SIGNS THAT YOUR CHILD'S HABIT HAS PROGRESSED INTO AN ADDICTION

- Isolation: spending excessive time alone in room or bathroom
- Change in mood: this is a possibility, but has to be evaluated on case by case basis
- Disinterested in spending time with others
- Excessively long periods of time in the shower
- Acting out behavior: sexting, sexual harassment, explicit emails, etc.
- Secrecy, relationship withdrawal
- Sexual behavior that is not developmentally appropriate
- A decreased satisfaction and ability to function well in relationships with friends, family members, and others.
- Symptoms of withdrawal/disengagement from family, friends and activities previously enjoyed. (Hoyt, 2015)
- Viewing multiple pornography sites. Any violent or extremely aberrant sites will create problems with healthy sexual development
- Engaging in risky behavior despite consideration of negative results: using school or church or neighbor's computers to look up porn
- Symptoms of withdrawal/disengagement from family, friends and activities previously enjoyed. (Hoyt, 2015)

14. IF YOUR CHILD HAS AN ADDICTION TO PORNOGRAPHY

If you have determined from the previous page that your child does indeed have an addiction, use the following to guide you through the next steps.

ACKNOWLEDGE THE ADDICTION

There needs to be ongoing, candid discussions about the nature of the addiction that your child initiates. This is often the most difficult step in the process of recovery and requires a sensitive and positive response. Your child should be commended for coming forth with such difficult information.

OFFER UNCONDITIONAL LOVE AND SUPPORT

Your child needs to know that you will be available to assist him or her no matter what the recovery process turns out to be. That means that you will remain supportive if relapses occur, which is likely.

EXPLORE TREATMENT OPTIONS

Look at a variety of options, including individual counseling and/or addiction recovery meetings. Your child should help choose a counselor who he or she will engage with, but your input is also necessary to ensure that the professional has the necessary credentials and experience to meet your child's needs. The therapist should also utilize a theoretical practice in line with your beliefs/values. If the child is young (under 12 years of age), the parent should have the responsibility of picking the therapist.

REFRAIN FROM MAKING YOUR CHILD FEEL ASHAMED

Shame and blame have no place in the recovery process. They are counterproductive to progress and will only sabotage your child's success in overcoming the addictive behavior.

EXPLORE EMOTIONAL NEEDS

What are the emotional needs being met by your child's involvement with pornography? Ask your child what prompted him or her to engage in viewing pornographic material for the first time. Was it to fill some emotional deficit? Did it work?

EXPLORE ALTERNATE, HEALTHY BEHAVIORS

What are healthy behaviors that could meet your child's emotional needs? Help your child to discover the variety of healthy, positive activities and hobbies that can satisfy one's emotional needs and contribute to one's emotional health.

RESPECT YOUR CHILD'S PRIVACY

This deeply personal issue should remain a private matter that is shared selectively and only with your child's permission. There needs to be a limited circle of people involved in the day-to-day dynamics of your child's recovery.

TEACH YOUR CHILD TO SELF-MONITOR

Self-monitoring is the ability to identify one's behaviors or tendencies and their triggers and to consider carefully before acting. This is a challenging task when children are typically impulsive and are looking for instant rewards, which has a strong link to addiction (see 21. Self-Monitoring). If working with a therapist, discuss with him ways to improve self-monitoring within your family.

CREATE A POSITIVE REINFORCEMENT SYSTEM

Validate your child's efforts and progress through a positive reinforcement system tailored to their needs (and that does not involve money or food). Incentives for positive behavior are powerful, and planning a special outing or activity as your child progresses can be a meaningful motivator for change.

CHECK IN

Be in constant touch with your child's feelings as he or she goes through the difficult process of overcoming an addiction. This process occurs one, small step at a time as you keep talking with your child, provide support, and establish accountability for his or her actions.

Walk beside your child as he or she takes this challenging journey to recovery and peace. Sharing this profound experience with your child will create a bond that will be extremely meaningful to both of you (Benson, 2015).

See our Resources section at the end of this book for professional counseling options or visit www.educateempowerkids.org for more resources and information about pornography and porn addiction.

15. COMMON PLACES FOR PORNOGRAPHY EXPOSURE

We cannot possibly protect or prepare our children for every circumstance. Mobile devices make it just as likely for our kids to see porn at church as at school. We can make sure our kids are well informed and prepared for various situations that may arise. Training your child to be ready in any setting is an unfortunate necessity, but one that parents are fully capable of doing.

SOCIAL MEDIA: Even with the best filters and spy ware, there is no way to filter social media sites like Twitter, Snapchat, Instagram, Tumblr, or Facebook. Even Pinterest has porn. A majority of kids are being exposed to porn through these apps through innocent searches, using clever emojis or hashtags in searches, the "Discover" function, by simply clicking on the search function, or being sent porn from friends through direct messaging. Although your teenager should experience social media before leaving home, they should be kept off of these platforms as long as possible--and definitely not before age 13. They do, however, need to use social media and make mistakes while still under your supervision and guidance.

HOME COMPUTER OR SMART PHONE: It is not unusual for a child to encounter porn through his or her home computer. Whether accidentally or on purpose, the simplest of searches can turn up pornographic results. Parents can place filters on home computers and personally monitor what kids are doing. Keeping computers in a public area like the kitchen or living room is the simplest step. Kids can be exposed at someone else's home, so discuss this concern with other parents.

SEXTING: (sending sexually explicit photographs or messages through cell phones) and messaging (emails, instant messaging through social media, etc.): If your child has a device that is capable of accessing the internet, it is definitely capable of sending and receiving messages through iMessage or a third party messaging app.

A teenager who takes a naked picture of him or herself and sends it to another teen has technically committed 3 felony crimes. He or she could be charged with promoting, distributing, and possessing child pornography. A teen who receives an explicit image (even if it was not requested) can be charged with possession. If the picture is sent to anyone, the teen may face distribution charges if caught. If convicted, the conviction will most likely be a felony and require the teenager to register as a sex offender (US Sexting Laws and Regulation, 2011).

SCHOOL COMPUTER: Kids in elementary school are taught computer skills as early as kindergarten. Although these computers and tablets have filters placed on them, images and sites commonly find a way "in." As teachers use YouTube and Google Image Search in the classroom, pornography exposure is becoming more common. This is why it's necessary to provide your child with a plan.

HOME ENTERTAINMENT SYSTEMS: Xbox, Playstation, Netflix, Amazon Streaming, Hulu, smart TVs–these are all easy and less-known ways for your child to be exposed to porn. Know how to place restrictions on these devices, learn how to place age restraints and a pin number on Netflix, and use YouTube for Kids.

//

DISCUSSION QUESTIONS

What would you do if a friend showed you pornography?

What would you do if pornography popped up on your computer at school?

What would you do if porn appeared on your cell phone?

What would you do if someone sent you a picture or video that was pornographic?

Do you know what can happen if you send/request/receive sexually explicit photos from someone else?

//

Media Literacy is the ability to analyze and evaluate media. Kids who are media literate can understand and think critically about the messages received from all forms of media, including sexualized media.

Most of us are media illiterate–adults as well as kids. We cannot instantly decode an image as quickly as we decode the written word. This illiteracy is alarming because kids are bombarded by images and ideas in the media they are exposed to every day. It's important for children to know that digitally enhanced images in the media show impossible standards that no one can attain. All media messages are constructed. Marketers and teams of advertisers put together campaigns for what people see and hear in the media. Often these campaigns are targeted toward kids, as in the case of porn.

📖 **Marketer:** *A person whose job is to promote, sell, or convince people to buy a product or service.*

WHY MEDIA LITERACY IS IMPORTANT

"Children are exposed to sexualization, violence, bullying, marketing of unhealthy foods, alcohol and tobacco, and unhealthy body images and gender stereotyping. Media consumption influences children's behavior and can contribute to aggression, violence and bullying, depression, body image issues, obesity, substance abuse, and other negative effects on physical and mental health" (Media Literacy Now, 2014). The only way to counteract all of these negative effects is to teach our children to look at what he or she is seeing with a critical eye.

READING AN IMAGE

Today's kids have to be more than "word" literate. Kids have to be able to read an image. Reading an image includes understanding the audience, context, and purpose of the image. Today's kids need to understand the underlying meaning an image portrays or what argument it's trying to make. A key part of reading an image includes deconstruction.

📖 **Deconstructing an Image:** *Breaking down the image or message into separate parts. (Words, images, body language, tone). Examining those parts critically and determining their individual meanings.*

FIND AN AD IN A MAGAZINE OR WATCH A COMMERCIAL ON TV. CHALLENGE KIDS TO ASK THE FOLLOWING QUESTIONS WHEN EXPOSED TO MEDIA

1. Who created the ad?

2. Who is the ad targeting? (What age group or type of person?)

3. What is the overall message of the ad?

4. Are there any underlying messages?

5. How does the ad make you feel? Does the ad make me feel like I need the product? That my life will be better with the product? Does it make me question my values or standards?

6. If there is a person in the ad, is he or she a realistic looking person?

7. Is this ad okay for kids?

Kids and teens have been exposed to media, both harmless and detrimental, their entire lives. Kids have a tendency to believe what they see and are told. The first step in helping them to be-come media literate is teaching them to think critically about the media they see. One of the best tools for this is teaching them how to deconstruct an image. If we can do this, our kids will be-come smart, well-informed media consumers.

For a great resource to teach your kids this important skill, check out *Petra's Power to See: A Media Literacy Adventure* available on Amazon or educateempowerkids.org.

17. TAKING INVENTORY AND CREATING A FAMILY GUIDELINE

HELP YOUR KIDS SEEK OUT THE BEST AND AVOID THE WORST

The point of taking inventory is to find out how much time and energy you and your family are actually spending with media. Not all media is bad, but there is definitive evidence that too much screen time is detrimental to brain development, growth, and relationships (Brown, et. al., 2015). While taking inventory, it's important to be honest with ourselves about just how much media we actually consume.

It is important to note the locations of all the devices in our home. These devices are like doors to our home. These doors can either be gateways to learning or vulnerable points where "intruders" can enter our home.

In your inventory, be sure to include your family's time spent with television, social media, and online, including video streaming sites like Netflix. Discuss any media that will NOT be allowed in your home such as shows that have violent or sexual content. Our kids are going to use various media throughout their lives: help your kids seek out the best and avoid the worst.

DISCUSSION QUESTIONS

What are our rules regarding games and TV ratings?

What rules should we have about our behavior online, especially on social media?

What are the consequences for breaking the rules?

What role does media play in our home? Is it the center of our attention, a tool, or is it used for occasional entertainment?

How much time do we want to spend on media?

HOUSEHOLD MEDIA GUIDELINE

Make a personalized, detailed guide and agreement within your family to determine what type of media, devices, timeframes, and protection tools will be used.

What to Include: Each family has to determine what their media guideline will contain based on their individual circumstances and needs. However, we suggest including the following:

TAKING INVENTORY

Our family's internet-enabled devices: _____

How many hours of screen time are we each using each day?

Name:_____ Hours: _____

Name:_____ Hours: _____

Name:_____ Hours: _____

Where do we keep our devices? _____

What video games/TV shows/social media are we using?

_____

SETTING LIMITS

What kind of media do we allow? _____

What are our screen time time limits? _____

What are our rules for social media? _____

What filters, parental controls, and/or accountability software will we use? _____

_____

Accountability and consequences: Your guideline should address these issues in order to work. You need to discuss how each family member will be accountable to the guideline as well as the consequences for breaking the rules. Make accountability part of the plan, but help your kids keep the rules by installing filters and restrictions. Talk about expectations for computer/phone use outside your home, and what websites or social media accounts are not allowed.

Adapted from Fight the New Drug's Family Media Standard, (2013). Retrieved April 25, 2015.

18. FULL ACCOUNTS AND DAILY CONNECTIONS

We all have several "accounts" that help us function and be happy and that are vital to our success. Here, we are focusing on the following accounts: physical, emotional, social, spiritual, and intellectual. In order to be happy and increase our well being, we need to maintain a certain "account balance."

Our kids face pressures that can readily deplete these accounts. It is our job to teach our kids awareness—what depletes these accounts and what we can do to fortify ourselves.

When one account is empty, we borrow from other accounts. For example, when a person feels lonely or upset, he may overeat to try to fill his account—borrowing from his physical account to fill his emotional account.

THE BEST WAY TO COMBAT THE DRAINING OF ACCOUNTS IS TO MAKE SURE WE DO A LITTLE BIT EACH DAY TO KEEP THEM FULL.

When several accounts are low, we experience anxiety, sadness, and even depression. In this state, kids are more vulnerable and prone to seek out unhealthy behaviors like viewing pornography, which can drain all of the accounts.

A pornography habit or addiction does not easily happen for someone who has purpose and meaning in their life. Nor does it easily happen to people who have deep connections within a family unit. The goal is to have daily interaction without screens to give kids ample opportunities to connect with parents. Creating deeper connections is one of the best addiction prevention tools we have.

The best way to combat the draining of accounts is to make sure we do a little bit each day to keep them full. Kids aren't always emotionally capable of understanding how one area of life can drain another, so a great way to explain this concept is with everyday instances or personal examples.

SOCIAL · INTELLECTUAL · SPIRITUAL · EMOTIONAL · PHYSICAL

DISCUSSION QUESTIONS

Have you noticed how when you don't get enough sleep you feel grumpy? (That's because your physical account isn't full and it's starting to pull from your emotional account.)

Sometimes when I've been watching TV too much, I start to feel irritable, especially when members of my family want to interact with me. Why do you think this is?

When I spend a lot of time on social media, I start to feel less of a need to interact with people in my real life. Is this a healthy habit?

When something is upsetting, is it healthier to cope by turning to a device to escape or by talking to a family member who can help you see things more positively?

Are online "relationships" just as fulfilling as those we have in real life? Can those fill our accounts?

Does someone sending you a "hug" online feel as good as receiving a hug from someone in person?

BETTER CHOICES

Many of us are beginning to disconnect from our neighbors and families and are turning more toward our online, shallower connections. This choice leads to a general disconnect in our communities and in society at large. Choosing to connect with family and friends in our real lives shows kids that the benefits of human connection outweigh online connection every time. We can teach them to do this daily:

> ⚜ Teach him or her to talk about issues with a friend or parent in person.

> ⚜ Your child is more important than a screen—if he or she feels neglected because of screens, teach them to ask those people they come into contact with to engage in human connection for a while.

> ⚜ Initiate screen-free times in your home. Have an idea of what you can do together. This will get everyone talking to each other and more comfortable with each other.

For a more in-depth instruction of helping kids to keep their accounts full, see Educate and Empower Kids' book *30 Days to a Stronger Child*.

19. HEALTHY SEXUAL INTIMACY

THE BEST, HEALTHIEST SEXUAL INTIMACY BUILDS FROM DEEP CONNECTION AND AFFECTION

One of the defining points of pornography is its total lack of intimacy. One person described porn as "sex without hands" (Gavrieli, n.d.). There is almost no hand holding, hugging, cuddling, caressing, or other behaviors associated with love, mutual respect, or deep connection. Because of this, it's imperative that we discuss the opposite of pornography: healthy sexual intimacy.

Often in media, and always in pornography, people are taught that sex and intimacy are separate concepts. Adults and kids are taught to suppress certain tender emotions, but to act upon any physical desires. Sexual education in school may discuss mechanics, but parents must take the lead on discussions of how to build intimacy and how to create great relationships. We must also model positive relationships to help our kids build healthy relationships and develop their own, unique, healthy sexuality.

As you discuss healthy sexual intimacy with your kids, address the following points in your conversations:

- Sex can be healthy and amazing!

- Intimacy (connecting with another human being) should be the focus of sex.

- Sex can be a positive or a negative experience: people can choose behaviors to make it positive.

- Sex works best when we understand our bodies: discuss puberty, body image, masturbation, mechanics of sex, and sexual identification.

- Sex needs to have clear consent from all involved.

- Sex can be unhealthy or dangerous when someone is manipulated or forced into sexual acts. (Talk about predators, grooming behaviors and what to do if he or she is in this situations.)

> IT'S IMPERATIVE THAT WE DISCUSS THE OPPOSITE OF PORNOGRAPHY: HEALTHY SEXUAL INTIMACY.

Healthy relationships create healthy sex. Discuss relationship concepts such as self-worth, boundaries, and healthy vs. abusive relationships. For great discussions about each of these topics and more, try our books, 30 *Days* of Sex Talks, Empowering Your Child with Knowledge of Sexual Intimacy (for ages 3-7, 8-11, and 12+). Healthy sexual intimacy is an important component to healthy relationships. However, because intimacy is often not portrayed accurately in media, we need to ensure our kids understand what intimacy is and how to build it in a relationship.

   ♛ Intimacy is a feeling of closeness, friendship, affection, love, and acceptance.

   ♛ Intimacy has emotional, mental, and social components, but can also have physical and spiritual components.

   ♛ Intimacy progresses over time, with the emotional and physical components sometimes progressing at different speeds. Physical intimacy may begin with hand holding or hugging and progress to caressing and beyond before emotional intimacy has increased.

   ♛ Understand how time together, physical affection, kindness, unselfishness, laughing and crying together, forgiving each other, and working through problems and accomplishing things together cultivates intimacy in a relationship.

DISCUSSION QUESTIONS

Why is adopting the viewpoint of sex and intimacy being two separate things a problem?

What happens when porn dictates your ideas about sex, instead of creating your own, unique sexuality?

Is it possible to develop your own unique sexuality without media or porn influence?

Can true intimacy happen "overnight" or within a few days?

How do you know if your relationship has intimacy?

Why is an intimate relationship satisfying?

Can you have an intimate relationship without a commitment?

20. MONITORING AND FILTERING

We all know that there are ways to monitor and filter online content, but sometimes it can be overwhelming to know where to start. However, monitoring and filtering are very important tools when it comes to protecting our kids against exposure to pornography. Everything is simpler when broken into manageable steps: take the time to educate yourself on the various monitoring and filtering options available to you.

MOBILE DEVICES

👑 There are filters and restrictions parents can set on tablets and any other mobile device. This is needful as these devices are by definition, mobile, and can be taken out of the home where router filtration would do no good. Mobile devices can use some of the same software applications used for computers to filter pornographic and other undesirable content.

👑 Most mobile carriers offer their own parental controls and services, which can be purchased for an additional fee.

👑 There is also the option to utilize built-in restrictions that are provided by some mobile manufacturers (Apple products, for instance). Educate and Empower Kids has provided step-by-step instructions for setting restrictions for iPhone on our site.

MANY PARENTS FEEL LIKE THEY'VE "TAKEN CARE OF THINGS" ONCE A FILTER IS INSTALLED. BUT BE HONEST WITH YOURSELF AND YOUR KIDS ABOUT ALL THAT CAN HAPPEN ON A DEVICE LEAVES YOUR HOUSE, ON ANY INTERNET-ENABLED DEVICE THAT ENTERS YOUR HOME, OR ON OTHERS' DEVICES.

HOME DEVICES

When it comes to filtering and monitoring Internet content within your home there are several points to concentrate on. Some filtering apps such as Circle have filtering at the router level in your home and some level of protection for mobile devices that your children take out of your home and connect to other Wireless Internet services.

THE ROUTER: The router is where the Internet first gets into the home. The router is the box that splits the Internet signal from the Internet service provider's (ISP) modem making it possible for all your devices to connect to the Internet. Sometimes the modem and router are built into one device that your ISP provides for you. OpenDNS is a free service that filters at the router level in your home.

WI-FI: Most of these connections are done wirelessly via Wi-Fi, which can be password restricted. There are also usually a few devices hard-wired directly to the router.

DEVICE FILTERING: There is also internet filtering at the device level, which means the actual computer, tablet or media device. There are many software applications out there that help to filter pornographic and other unwanted content. Some examples are: K9Webprotection.com, Netnanny.com, Covenanteyes.com, and many others. Research your options by looking at the features and deciding what your priorities are and what best fits your needs.

ACCOUNTABILITY SOFTWARE: Accountability Software is not a filter and does not block content. Internet accountability is a report of what you see and do online, designed to start a conversation, helping everyone in your home make wiser choices about internet use. For parents, it means you can have targeted conversations about the sites your kids visit and the search terms being used (Internet Accountability Software for Windows, Mac, and Mobile, 2015).

Remember, these methods really only act as band-aids and cannot replace discussion and true accountability. Your child will leave your house one day, and at that point he or she will need to make their own healthy choices. The process of monitoring and filtering should start at a young age and progress to allow your child a bit more freedom where you see fit, always including a discussion of the underlying purpose. This way, your child won't feel bombarded with all that is out there when he or she leaves your home. Done correctly, these steps will prepare kids to make good choices on their own, even when no one is looking.

21. SELF-MONITORING

📖 **Self-monitoring:** *The ability to identify one's behaviors or tendencies and their triggers and to consider carefully before acting.*

Our kids won't always live under our roofs. When teens leave for college and progress into adulthood, we want them to avoid pornography for the rest of their lives. Kids need to be well informed and know the specific harmful effects of porn, not just that "it's bad." As kids come to understand how addiction works, they can also be taught that their brains have great power and have the ability to make good choices. Teens need not be slaves to every desire or emotion that pops into their heads.

As you discuss self-monitoring as a skill, remind your child of the **R-U-N** plan developed earlier in this book, and talk about ways to deal with various, specific scenarios that may occur in their future, for example:

🗨 What should you say if your friend wants to show you pornography on the school bus?

🗨 What should you do if a pornographic image pops up while you are doing your homework?

🗨 What can you do or whom can you talk to if you have questions about sex or pornography?

🗨 Is it still important to avoid pornography as an adult, when you are away from home?

Another meaningful part of self-monitoring is trust. We must give our kids the tools and information (such as the lessons in this book) to succeed and then convey to our kids that we trust them to make good decisions. It can be very empowering for a child to be trusted and given the opportunities to succeed or fail at this.

It is also important that you have ongoing discussions about pornography, sexual intimacy, internet activities, relationships with friends and peers, and other topics important to your child. These ongoing talks should be layered (take place repeatedly) and should mature and grow over time. This will give greater protection and preparation to our kids who do, or will, spend a large majority of their future time online.

An ongoing dialogue about their emotional health is also important. Your kids should understand how emotions can drive impulsive, last-minute decisions, many of which are not healthy. Often when we are stressed, angry, tired, depressed, or sad we seek out things that can harm us, like pornography. Discuss coping mechanisms on occasion (or when you observe something you are concerned about) to help kids identify their personal coping skills and help direct them toward healthy coping skills (see 9. Pornography is Addictive and 18. Full Accounts and Daily Connections).

DISCUSSION QUESTIONS

Sometimes a pornographic image we come upon may feel "stuck" in our heads long after we have turned off the computer or phone. How can we distract ourselves or replace that image?

What are situations in your life that are stressful or sad that may trigger your emotions in a negative way or cause you to seek out unhealthy things?

If you are having a tough day or are bored and want to see something online that you know you shouldn't, what are some other things you can do to distract yourself from wanting to go online? (read, ride a bike, talk with friends, take a nap, make something, draw, play a sport)

Who can you talk to when life is difficult?

Remind your kids that you love them and that he or she can talk with you about anything. This way, the need to self-monitor isn't placed completely on the child's shoulders—he or she can talk it out with a parent as well. As kids mature and get ready to leave home, they'll be better equipped to handle their own self-monitoring.

22. PORN DESTROYS

At its core, pornography teaches that sex is adversarial, narcissistic, and humiliating. After you strip away the excuses that it is just a fun, playful fantasy, the real message and meanings that are taught to our kids can be seen (Layden, 2010). Use the following topics to spark discussion with your teenagers.

PORN TEACHES THAT INTIMACY IS IRRELEVANT

As we have mentioned before, there is no loving embrace, no tender words, or thoughtful love-making in pornography. There is only an empty sexual act (see 19. Healthy Sexual Intimacy). The constant portrayal of people selfishly fixating on their own pleasure teaches kids that sex is something you take from someone, not something you give together.

PORN NORMALIZES DEVIANT BEHAVIOR

"People construct their notions of reality from the media they consume, and the more consistent and coherent the message, the more people believe it to be true" (Dines, 2015). This is what is so alarming about popular genres right now and what is being produced over and over again by pornographers. The porn industry has created a very consistent and coherent message about women. The message being that women like to be coerced into sex, should be raped, and the younger they are the better. "Teen" porn, where women portraying young teenage girls have sex with older men, also normalizes the idea that men should want to have sex with and should have access to underage girls. Another deviant behavior that is celebrated in porn is incest with many "mom," "step-mom" and "step-sister" themes rising in the top search results.

PORN CELEBRATES MALE DOMINATION

"The majority of the pornography that saturates our hyper-mediated lives presents not images of 'just sex,' but sex in the context of male dominance" (Jensen, 2011). There is a consistent, perpetual theme in porn: that of a man or several men placing a woman in a position of powerlessness. She is usually on her knees or pushed down in some way. This emphasis on male dominance twists and perverts healthy sexual dynamics between the sexes.

> **THE CONSTANT PORTRAYAL OF PEOPLE SELFISHLY FIXATING ON THEIR OWN PLEASURE TEACHES KIDS THAT SEX IS SOMETHING YOU TAKE FROM SOMEONE, NOT SOMETHING YOU GIVE TOGETHER.**

DISCUSSION QUESTIONS

Why doesn't porn depict loving, intimate behavior?

Do you think children are born with a desire to dominate others or is this sometimes socialized into them through media and pornography?

Why is it so easy to believe most of the things we read? Why is it so easy to believe what we see in a video?

Does the number of times we watch something effect our beliefs? If I watch several people smile while being slapped, will I start to believe they like it?

If I see repeated videos of actors and actresses portraying fathers and daughters who want to have sex with one another, will I start to see this behavior as normal?

Some experts (Dines, 2010) argue that porn hijacks our sexuality by relentlessly telling us what sex "ought" to be. Should a person create his own unique, healthy sexuality without influence from media or porn? Or does he need "help" from these outside influences?

23. PORNOGRAPHY FUELS HATE

Because of its harsh, callous nature, porn does more damage to an individual's mind than any other substance or media one can consume. Its pervasive use among kids and adults is changing the way we see each other and the way we treat one another.

PORN DEHUMANIZES PEOPLE

It's important to note that a woman is never called a woman in pornography. She is called a whore, a slut, or much worse. By treating the woman with disrespect and contempt, the porn user can easily forget she is a human being. She then can be seen as an object to be used and thrown away. This appears to be done on purpose by some pornographers. This way, the user won't see the actress as any relatable woman he knows (his sister, mother, girlfriend). Instead, he can see her as a "slut" who wants or enjoys being brutalized or coerced into an act (Dines, 2010).

PORN IS VIOLENT

On every site and in every genre there is an unlimited supply of videos where a woman is called cruel names, spit on, choked, slapped, ejaculated on, coerced into sex, or raped. A popular theme is a woman who is coerced into sex or raped, but seems to enjoy her maltreatment. These more violent and humiliating videos used to be rare, but are so popular now, they can be found within three to four clicks online.

PORN IS RACIST

Every negative cultural, or racial stereotype is accepted and played up in pornography. From Latinos and Asians, to Blacks and Middle Easterners, if you are a minority, you will be stereotyped and demeaned. Asians are usually portrayed as petite, submissive girls who are looking for a man to tell them what to do, while Latinas are portrayed as illegal immigrants or maids who will do anything to please.

PORN DESTROYS EMPATHY

In pornography, sex happens with no concern for others, thus teaching a total lack of empathy for others. Often, the man's behavior in porn seems sociopathic (without a conscience) and even sadistic—simulating forced sex or rape. More confusion for kids and teens results when the actress acts like she is enjoying her humiliation or coercion. This can lead to the user—of any age—to believe she "likes" what is happening to her and even "wants" to be raped.

"Pornography is one way that men's capacity for empathy can be dramatically diminished" (Jensen, 2011). It discourages the ability to imagine what another human being might be feeling. "Pornography has always presented women as objectified bodies for male sexual pleasure, but each year pornography does that with more overt cruelty toward women. The 'gonzo' genre of pornography, where the industry pushes the culture's limits with the most intense sexual degradation, encourages men to see women as vehicles for their sexual pleasure, even depicting women as eager to participate in their own degradation" (Jensen, 2011).

DISCUSSION QUESTIONS

What happens when we refuse to call a man a "man" or a woman a "woman"? Why did the Nazi's never call Jewish people "human beings"?

Why does violence seem to "disappear" when it is combined with sex? Why do we accept that the woman must "want it" or "like it" (slapping, name-calling) if sex is involved?

Why are racism and cultural stereotypes celebrated in pornography, when they are generally rejected in all other areas of pop culture?

What does it mean for us as a society that a majority of boys
(and girls) are watching cruel, violent pornography as a means of sex education?

24. THE TRAFFICKING CONNECTION

In the sex trade, pornography, prostitution, and sex trafficking are the same. More than 80% of the time, women in the sex industry are under pimp control—which IS trafficking. Pornography meets the legal definition of trafficking if the pornographer recruits, entices, or obtains women for the purpose of photographing sex (Farley, 2015).

According to Melissa Farley (2011), the conditions leading to entry into pornography are much the same as conditions leading women to enter into prostitution. These include: poverty, vulnerable or deceptive job offers, lack of educational and job training opportunities, and childhood physical and sexual abuse.

A vast majority of women choose to be in pornography because it's the best of very few options. Many times these women are choosing between poverty and a job in the sex industry. They do not choose this work simply because they just love sex or because they are dying to share their body and bedroom talents with the world. Many are coerced, some are lured by the idea of quick money, and many have to use drugs or alcohol to cope with unique physical and mental demands of their work.

In the porn industry, pimps have the more dignified title of "manager," but their work is the same. Many ex-porn actresses say their "managers" find work for their charges, give them drugs when they cannot cope from the horrors of their job, and coerce them to do certain acts that they would otherwise find reprehensible (Stutler, 2011).

Legal pornography is not the only form of porn that saw a huge market increase with the advent of the Internet: child pornography has also increased at a disturbing rate. This increase has led to a rise in child porn trafficking over the years. It is now far easier for images to be trafficked online without leaving a trail.

For many trafficked women and children all over the world, pornography is used as a training tool. Victims are shown pornography in order to teach them what they are to perform with clients. This is especially relevant as many porn users expect to recreate the acts they seen online.

We must understand: pornography is not harmless. It leaves victims as it is made and consumed. Avoiding pornography helps stop the demand for legal and child pornography.

DISCUSSION QUESTIONS

Why is pornography legal when prostitution is not (in most countries)?

Can you see any major differences between pornography and prostitution?

Do porn actresses and actors deserve our contempt or our compassion?

What can we do help people who have been trafficked?

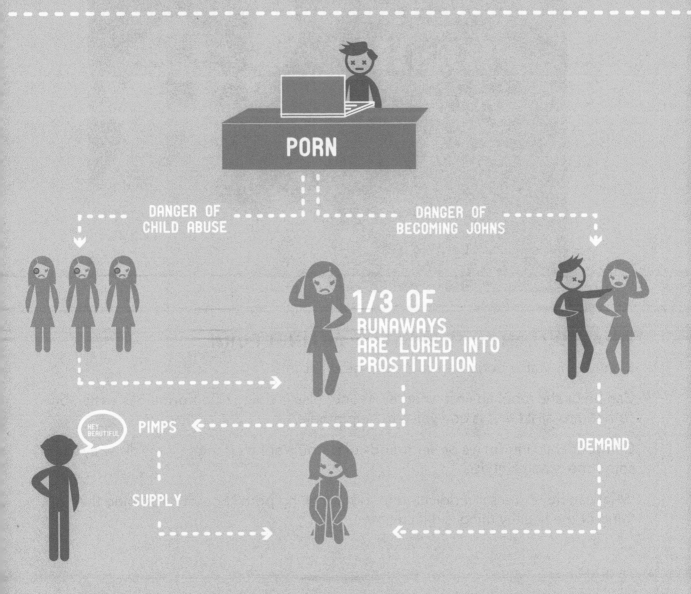

25. RELATED TOPICS TO DISCUSS WITH OLDER KIDS/TEENS

WILL POP CULTURE CATCH UP TO SCIENCE?

The research is pouring in: porn use is unhealthy, addictive, and harmful to individuals, families, and society. But pop culture still depicts porn use as normal, harmless fun. The same held true for cigarette use for decades. Research showed that tobacco could kill you, but movies and television still celebrated its use until people demanded better of those industries. Let's work to change this!

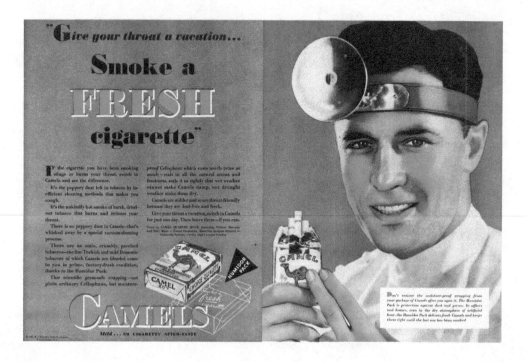

WHAT YOU CAN DO TO SPEAK UP AGAINST PORN

Many teens watch porn. Can your teen be different?

Can he or she rebel against what "everyone" else is doing? Conforming is easier, but sometimes all it takes is one voice to help others.

Can your child inform his or her friends of pornography's dangers or walk away when someone is watching it?

What can he or she say if ridiculed for not watching porn? Sometimes doing the right thing or the healthy thing is difficult.

SEXTING

When anyone sends a naked/barely-clothed photo of a person under 18 years of age, that is distributing child pornography. When someone sends sexual comments to another person, it can be construed as sexual harassment. Discuss with your child the emotional and legal consequences of such behavior.

MASTURBATION

An open, honest conversation about masturbation can be really helpful to your kids, especially since it usually accompanies porn viewing. If you have views that masturbation is healthy or unhealthy, discuss these with your kids.

SELF-MONITORING AS A TEEN

With or without our filtering and monitoring capabilities, our teenagers will experience a wide variety of innapropriate images, before they leave our homes, especially if they are using social media. Before your teenager moves out of your house discuss ways they can stay safe and porn-free after they leave your home. Discuss the myriad of other coping mechanisms they can use when they are bored, lonely, stressed, or even just curious.

We discuss these topics in greater detail in our books, 30 Days of Sex Talks, Empowering Your Child with Knowledge of Sexual Intimacy and 30 Days to a Stronger Child.

26. RELATED TOPICS TO DISCUSS WITH KIDS OF ALL AGES

RESPECT FOR SELF AND OTHERS

A healthy sense of self-worth is a powerful deterrent to pornography. If your child feels good about him or herself and views others as valuable and deserving of respect, he or she is much less likely to be caught in the porn trap. They will be less likely to want to see people objectified and degraded (Andrews, 2014).

CONNECTING IN REAL LIFE VS. ELECTRONIC CONNECTIONS

With all the ways to connect through social media, texting and email, it can actually isolate us, removing face-to-face interactions. If our main interactions are behind screens, it can cultivate a sense of other people being two-dimensional and emotionally removed. This disconnect can desensitize us and our kids to other people. We need to teach the value of relationships in real life!

BODY IMAGE

As our kids experience hyper sexualized media and pornography, he or she will encounter countless images of unattainable, computerized "beauty" that will make them feel inferior. It is therefore, imperative to discuss healthy body image and loving your body as it is.

HEALTHY RELATIONSHIPS/BOUNDARIES

Media often portrays poor relationships and ineffective boundaries. Make sure your child understands what a good relationship looks like, what sacrifices it takes, and how to create one.

BODILY INTEGRITY

Our bodies are the storehouse of our humanity and should be honored as such. Teach your child through your words and example that his body is special and worth protecting.

PREDATORS USE PORNOGRAPHY FOR GROOMING

It's a fact; predators use pornography as a grooming tool to desensitize their victims and to show their victims what they want performed. You child must understand that no one (especially an adult or older kid) should show them pornography.

In our books 30 Days of Sex Talks: Empowering Your Child with Knowledge of Sexual Intimacy and 30 Days to a Stronger Child, we cover these subjects in greater detail.

EDUCATEEMPOWERKIDS

IF YOU ENJOYED THIS BOOK, PLEASE LEAVE A POSITIVE REVIEW ON AMAZON.COM

For great resources and information,
follow us on our social media outlets:

Facebook: www.facebook.com/educateempowerkids/

Twitter: @EduEmpowerKids

Pinterest: pinterest.com/educateempower/

Instagram: Eduempowerkids

Subscribe to our website for exclusive offers and information at:
www.educateempowerkids.org

RESOURCES

If you are a parent, teacher, or concerned adult looking to help children and teens, these are great websites and organizations for you to use as resources:

Educate and Empower Kids

Educate and Empower Kids provides resources to parents to encourage connection and healthy relationships. We fight pornography by promoting healthy sexuality education, family connection, and media literacy. www.educateempowerkids.org

Follow us on our social media outlets:

Facebook: www.facebook.com/educateempowerkids/

Twitter: @EduEmpowerKids

Pinterest: pinterest.com/educateempower/

Instagram: Eduempowerkids

Protect Young Minds

Protect Young Minds provides practical solutions for raising resilient kids in the digital age. They mentor parents with tools to prevent pornography addiction, effective ways to respond to exposure and use, and training on how to change the world by spreading the word.

www.protectyoungminds.org

If you have a teenager, this is a great organization for them:

Fight the New Drug

If you have found that your child is struggling with pornography use, the Fortify Program is a great step toward recovery. It is free for anyone from ages 13-18, and it breaks it down in a language and style easy to understand.

www.fightthenewdrug.org

If you are interested in getting involved in the fight against pornography as an advocate or an educator, these are effective websites and organizations:

National Center on Sexual Exploitation

The National Center on Sexual Exploitation changes corporate and government policies that facilitate sexual exploitation by empowering the public and uniting leaders in the movement.

www.endsexualexploitation.org

White Ribbon Week

White Ribbon Week is a positive school program presented by volunteers or teachers that helps kids make healthy choices in media and technology. Every day, kids learn a new principle of online behavior—reinforced through discussions and fun activities. This program is research based and kid tested.

www.whiteribbonweek.org

If you or your spouse has an addiction to pornography, these websites and organizations provide useful resources:

Betrayal Trauma Recovery

Betrayal Trauma Recovery is a non-profit that helps women face their husband's porn use and related behaviors—lies, emotional abuse—with support and confidence. Check out the Betrayal Trauma Recovery checklist for women who discover pornography on their husband's phone or elsewhere, or have conversations that leave them confused and suspicious. The free BTR provides live, online, daily group sessions and individual sessions with certified professionals to lead women to safety and save them from years of pain and confusion.

www.btr.org

Addo Recovery

The symptoms of betrayal trauma are many. Addo Recovery empowers women everywhere to know that it's not their fault, they're not alone, and they can find peace again.

www.addorecovery.com

SA Lifeline

SA Lifeline Foundation is a non-profit 501c3 organization dedicated to Recovering Individuals and Healing Families from the effects of sexual addiction and betrayal trauma. They provide education and therapeutic resources for those facing addiction and their partners.

www.salifeline.org

LifeStar

For over 20 years, LifeStar has been helping individuals, spouses, and families heal from the devastating effects of pornography addiction and other sexually compulsive behaviors.

www.lifestarnetwork.com

CITATIONS

"Addiction." Random House Kernerman Webster's College Dictionary, © 2010 K Dictionaries Ltd. Copyright 2005, 1997, 1991 by Random House, Inc. All rights reserved.

Alexander, D. (2016, March 07). Porn Industry Trends—Where Will They Target Your Children Next? Retrieved September 1, 2018, from https://educateempowerkids.org/porn-industry-trends-for-2016/

Anderson, C. (2011). The Impact of Pornography on Children, Youth, and Culture. Near Press.

Anderson, C. (2015). "Why Pornography is a Public Health Issue." In Pornography: A Public Health Crisis. Symposium conducted by the National Center on Sexual Exploitation in Washington D.C.

Andrews, C. (2014, May 1). "8 Ways You Can Fight Porn Beyond Talking About It." Educate Empower Kids. Retrieved December 1, 2015, from http://educateempowerkids.org/take_action_post/3rd-newest-take-action-educate-article-title-link-goes-3/.

Benson, M. (2015, February 2). "What to Look for When Choosing An Addiction Therapist for Your Child." Educate Empower Kids. Retrieved December 9, 2015, from http://educateempowerkids.org/resources/look-choosing-therapist-child/.

Braun-Courville, D. K., and M. Rojas. (2009). "Exposure to Sexually Explicit Web Sites and Adolescent Sexual Attitudes and Behaviors." Journal of Adolescent Health, 45(2), 156–62. (p. 157).

Bridges, A., R. Wosnitzer, E. Scharrer, C. Sun, and R. Liberman. (2010). "Aggression and Sexual Behavior in Best-Selling Pornography Videos: A Content Analysis Update." Violence Against Women, 1065–85.

Brown, A., Shifrin, D., & Hill, D. (2015, September 28). Beyond 'turn it off': How to advise families on media use. Retrieved December 23, 2015, from http://www.aappublications.org/content/36/10/54.full.

Ciotti, G. (n.d.). "Supernormal Stimuli: Your Brain On Porn, Junk Food, and the Internet." Re-trieved October 20, 2015, from http://lifehacker.com/supernormal-stimuli-is-your-brain-built-for-porn-junk-1575846913?.

Dines, G. (2010). Pornland: How Porn has Hijacked Our Sexuality. Boston: Beacon Press.

Dines, G. (2012, November 16). Presentation at the Nova Scotia Women's Summit. Retrieved from https://www.youtube.com/watch?v=-Z5iANEfQUU.

Dines, G. (2015). "Today's Pornography and the Crisis of Violence Against Women and Chil-dren." In Pornography: A Public Health Crisis. Symposium conducted by the National Center on Sexual Exploitation in Washington D.C.

Doidge, N. (n.d.). News. Retrieved November 1, 2015, from http://hungarianreview.com/article/20140706_sex_on_the_brain_what_brain_plasticity_teaches_about_internet_porn.

Drawing the Connection Between Media Literacy and Health. (2014). Retrieved December 8, 2015, from http://medialiteracynow.org/wp-content/uploads/2014/01/Drawing-the-connection-between-Media-Literacy-and-Public-Health.pdf.

Farley, M. (2011). "Pornography is Infinite Prostitution." In Big Porn Inc. North Melbourne: Spinifex Press Pty.

Farley, M. (2015). "Pornography, Prostitution, and Trafficking: Making the Connections." In Pornography: A Public Health Crisis. Symposium conducted by the National Center on Sexual Exploitation in Washington D.C.

Family Media Standard. Fight the New Drug (2015). Retrieved December 9, 2015, from http://fightthenewdrug.org/family-media-standard/.

Gavrieli, R. (n.d.). "Why I Stopped Watching Porn: Ran Gavrieli at TEDxJaffa 2013." Video at TEDxTalks. Retrieved November 13, 2015, from http://tedxtalks.ted.com/video/Why-I-Stopped-Watching-Porn-Ran;search:why i stopped.

Hilton, D. (2015). "Pornography and the Brain: Public Health Considerations." In Pornography: A Public Health Crisis. Symposium conducted by the National Center on Sexual Exploitation in Washington D.C.

Hoyt, L. (2015, February 15). "Signs and Symptoms of Porn Addiction in Kids." Educate Empower Kids. Retrieved December 9, 2015, from http://educateempowerkids.org/resources/signs-of-porn-addiction-in-kids/.

"Internet Accountability Software for Windows, Mac, and Mobile." (2015). Retrieved December 9, 2015, from http://www.covenanteyes.com/services/internet-accountability/.

Jensen, R. (2011, August 11). "Pornography Is What the End of the World Looks Like." Re-trieved October 28, 2015, from http://goodmenproject.com/featured-content/pornography-is-what-the-end-of-the-world-looks-like/.

Kemmet, D. (n.d.). Who is More Important to Teens-Parents or Peers? Retrieved December 23, 2015, from https://www.ag.ndsu.edu/mercercountyextension/news/around-the-home/who-is-more-important-to-teens-parents-or-peers.

Layden, M. (2004). "Committee on Commerce, Science, and Transportation, Subcommittee on Science and Space, U.S. Senate, Hearing on the Brain Science Behind Pornography Addiction." Retrieved November 25, 2015, from http://www.ccv.org/wp-content/uploads/2010/04/Judith_Reisman_Senate_Testimony-2004.11.18.pdf.

Layden, M. (2010). "Pornography and Violence: A New Look at Research." Retrieved Novem-ber 11, 2015, from http://www.socialcostsofpornography.com/Layden_Pornography_and_Violence.pdf.

Morris, C. (n.d.). "Things Are Looking Up in America's Porn Industry." NBC News. Retrieved November 24, 2015, from http://www.nbcnews.com/business/business-news/things-are-looking-americas-porn-industry-n289431.

"The Nanny Notes." (n.d.). Retrieved November 16, 2015, from https://www.netnanny.com/blog/the-detrimental-effects-of-pornography-on-small-children/.

(n.d.). Retrieved November 10, 2015, from http://www.nsvrc.org/sites/default/files/publications_nsvrc_factsheet_impact-of-exposure-to-sexually-explicit-and-eploitative-materials.pdf.

"Pitt Researchers Find Adolescent Brains Over-Process Rewards, Suggesting Root of Risky Behavior, Psychological Disorders". (2011). Retrieved December 4, 2015, from http://www.news.pitt.edu/news/Moghaddam-teen-brains-reward.

"Porn Changes the Brain." (n.d.). Retrieved November 24, 2015, from http://www.fightthenewdrug.org/porn-changes-the-brain/.

Rosenzweig, J. (2013, October). "What's the Impact of Porn on Kids?" Philly.com. Retrieved from http://www.philly.com/philly/blogs/healthy_kids/Whats-the-impact-of-porn-on-kids.html.

Stiffelman, S. (2011, August). "My Son Saw Sexually Explicit Material Online—What Should I Do?" huffingtonpost.com. Retrieved from http://www.huffingtonpost.com/2011/08/08/safety-on-internet-sexually-explicit-material_n_918353.html.

Stutler, A. (2011). "The Connections Between Pornography and Sex Trafficking." Retrieved December 5, 2015, from http://richmondjusticeinitiative.com/the-connections-between-pornography-and-sex-trafficking/.

Owens, E., R. Behun, J. Manning, and R. Reid. (2012). "The Impact of Internet Pornography on Adolescents: A Review of the Research." Sexual Addiction and Compulsivity, vol. 19, no. 1-2: 99-122.

"Ten Reasons Why You Need To Talk To Your Child About Porn." Educate Empower Kids. (2015, March 13). Retrieved November 7, 2015, from http://educateempowerkids.org/ten-reasons-why-you-to-talk-to-your-child-about-pornography/.

"U.S. Sexting Laws and Regulations." (2011). Retrieved December 8, 2015, from http://mobilemediaguard.com/state_main.html.

Weiss, LCSW, CSAT-S, R. (2015, June 9). The Prevalence of Porn. Retrieved December 23, 2015, from http://blogs.psychcentral.com/sex/2013/05/the-prevalence-of-porn/.

Wilson, G. (n.d.). "Your Brain on Porn: How Internet Porn Affects the Brain." (2015, May). Re-trieved October 24, 2015, from http://yourbrainonporn.com/your-brain-on-porn-series.

Printed in July 2022
by Rotomail Italia S.p.A., Vignate (MI) - Italy